Album of Negro Spirituals

Newly Adapted and Arranged by J. Rosamond Johnson

CONTENTS	Page
DE BAND O'GIDEON	26
DEEP RIVER	38
DIDN'T MY LORD DELIVER DANIEL?	10
EV'RY TIME I FEEL DE SPIRIT	42
EZEKIEL SAW DE WHEEL	35
GIMME DAT OLD TIME RELIGION	50
GIT ON BO'D LITTLE CHILDREN	21
GO DOWN MOSES	6
GOIN' TO SHOUT ALL OVER GOD'S HEAB'N	54
I BEEN IN DE STORM, SO LONG	22
I COULDN'T HEAR NOBODY PRAY	46
I'M A-ROLLIN'	52
JOSHUA FIT THE BATTLE O' JERICO	18
LIS'EN TO DE LAM'S	44
LIT'LE DAVID PLAY ON YO' HARP	14
NOBODY KNOWS DE TROUBLE I SEE	4
NOW LET ME FLY	41
O, ROCKS DON'T FALL ON ME	32
PETER, GO RING-A DEM BELLS	30
PETER ON DE SEA, SEA, SEA, SEA	48
ROLL JORDAN ROLL	12
SOMETIMES I FEEL LIKE A MOTHERLESS CHILD	24
STANDIN' IN THE NEED OF PRAYER	8
STEAL AWAY TO JESUS	16
SWING LOW SWEET CHARIOT	2
WERE YOU THERE WHEN THEY CRUCIFIED MY LORD?	28

A Publication of

EDWARD B. MARKS MUSIC COMPANY

EXCLUSIVELY DISTRIBUTED BY
HAL•LEONARD CORPORATION

7777 W. BLUEMOUND RD. P.O. BOX 13819 MILWAUKEE, WI 53213

Swing Low Sweet Chariot

Adapted and arranged by
J. ROSAMOND JOHNSON
a.s.c.a.p.

Copyright © 1940 by Edward B. Marks Music Company   Copyright Renewed
International Copyright Secured   Made in U.S.A.   All Rights Reserved
Used by Permission

Go Down Moses

Adapted and arranged by
J. ROSAMOND JOHNSON
a.s.c.a.p.

Copyright © 1940 by Edward B. Marks Music Company   Copyright Renewed
International Copyright Secured   Made in U.S.A.   All Rights Reserved
Used by Permission

Standin' In The Need Of Prayer

Adapted and arranged by
J. ROSAMOND JOHNSON
a.s.c.a.p.

Copyright © 1940 by Edward B. Marks Music Company   Copyright Renewed
International Copyright Secured   Made in U.S.A.   All Rights Reserved
Used by Permission

Roll Jordan Roll

Adapted and arranged by
J. ROSAMOND JOHNSON
a.s.c.a.p.

Copyright © 1940 by Edward B. Marks Music Company Copyright Renewed
International Copyright Secured   Made in U.S.A.   All Rights Reserved
Used by Permission

Lit'le David Play On Yo' Harp

Adapted and arranged by
J. ROSAMOND JOHNSON
a.s.c.a.p.

STEAL AWAY TO JESUS

Adapted and arranged by
J. ROSAMOND JOHNSON
a. s. c. a. p.

Copyright © 1940 by Edward B. Marks Music Company   Copyright Renewed
International Copyright Secured   Made in U.S.A.   All Rights Reserved
Used by Permission

Joshua Fit The Battle O' Jerico

Copyright © 1940 by Edward B. Marks Music Company   Copyright Renewed
International Copyright Secured   Made in U.S.A.   All Rights Reserved
Used by Permission

20

Git On Bo'd Little Child'en

Adapted and arranged by
J. ROSAMOND JOHNSON
a. s. c. a. p.

I Been In De Storm, So Long

De Band O' Gideon

Adapted and arranged by
J. ROSAMOND JOHNSON
a. s. c. a. p.

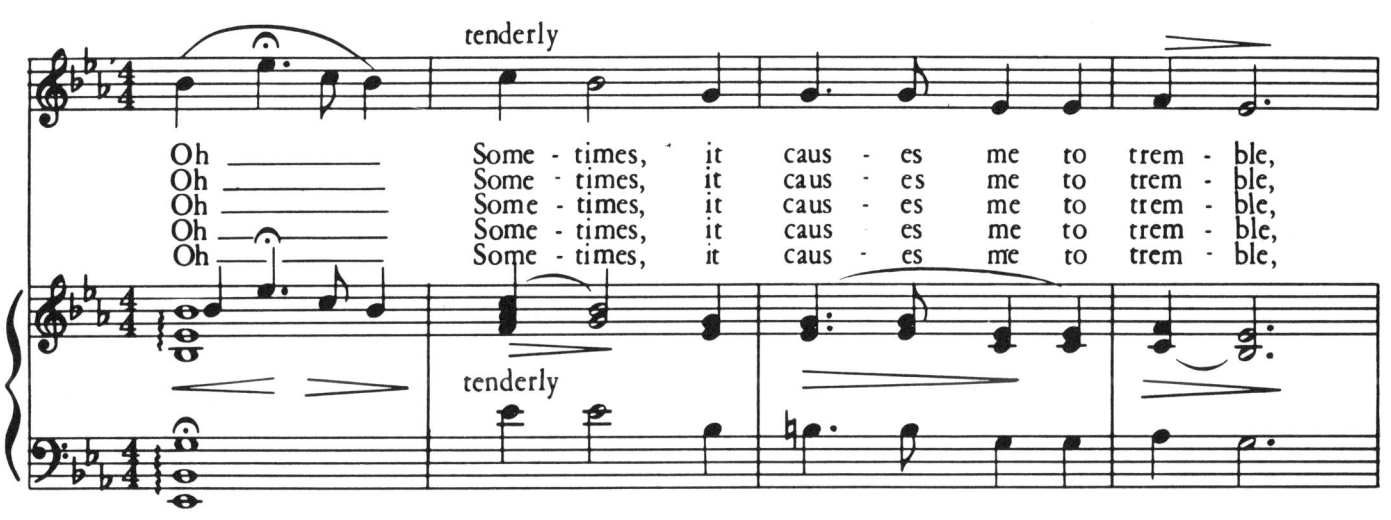

Peter, Go Ring-a Dem Bells

Adapted and arranged by
J. ROSAMOND JOHNSON
a.s.c.a.p.

O, Rocks Don't Fall On Me

Adapted and arranged by
J. ROSAMOND JOHNSON
a.s.c.a.p.

Copyright © 1940 by Edward B. Marks Music Company   Copyright Renewed
International Copyright Secured   Made in U.S.A.   All Rights Reserved
Used by Permission

Ezekiel Saw De Wheel

Adapted and arranged by
J. ROSAMOND JOHNSON
a. s. c. a. p.

Now Let Me Fly

Adapted and arranged by
J. ROSAMOND JOHNSON
a. s. c. a. p.

Copyright © 1940 by Edward B. Marks Music Company
International Copyright Secured Made in U.S.A.
Used by Permission

Copyright Renewed
All Rights Reserved

Lis'en To De Lam's

Adapted and arranged by
J. ROSAMOND JOHNSON
a. s. c. a. p.

Copyright © 1940 by Edward B. Marks Music Company   Copyright Renewed
International Copyright Secured   Made in U.S.A.   All Rights Reserved
Used by Permission

I Couldn't Hear Nobody Pray

Adapted and arranged by
J. ROSAMOND JOHNSON
a. s. c. a. p.

Copyright © 1940 by Edward B. Marks Music Company   Copyright Renewed
International Copyright Secured   Made in U.S.A.   All Rights Reserved
Used by Permission

Peter On De Sea, Sea, Sea, Sea.

Adapted and arranged by
J. ROSAMOND JOHNSON
a.s.c.a.p.

49

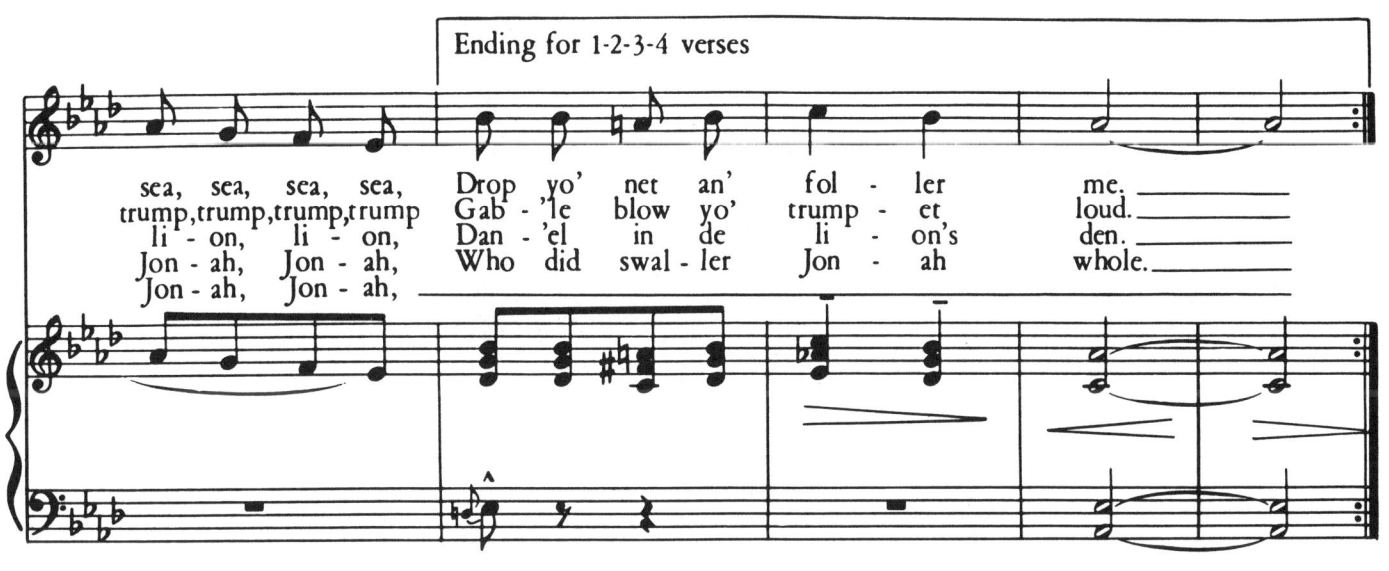

Gimme Dat Old Time Religion

Adapted and arranged by
J. ROSAMOND JOHNSON
a.s.c.a.p.

I'm A-Rollin'

Adapted and arranged by
J. ROSAMOND JOHNSON
a. s. c. a. p.

Moderato
With steady swing

I'm a-rol-lin', I'm a-rol-lin' I'm a rol-lin' through an un-friend-ly world. I'm a-rol-lin' I'm a-rol-lin' through an un-friend-ly world. I'm a-world.

O, broth-ers won't you help me, O, broth-ers won't you
O, sis-ters won't you help me, O, sis-ters won't you

Copyright © 1940 by Edward B. Marks Music Company   Copyright Renewed
International Copyright Secured   Made in U.S.A.   All Rights Reserved
Used by Permission

Goin' To Shout All Over God's Heab'n

Adapted and arranged by
J. ROSAMOND JOHNSON
a.s.c.a.p.

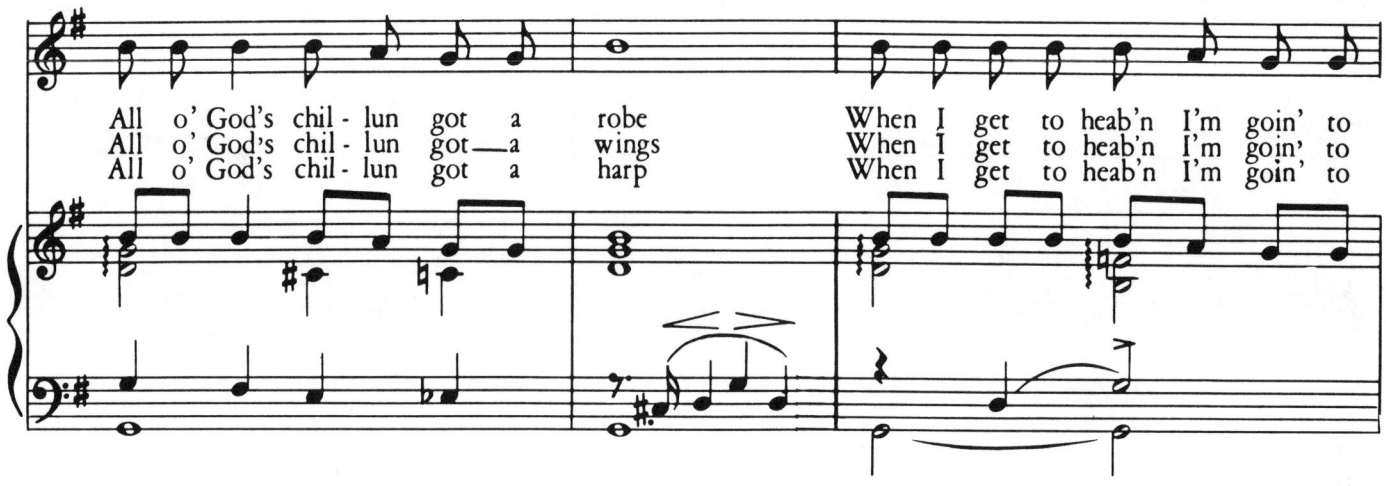

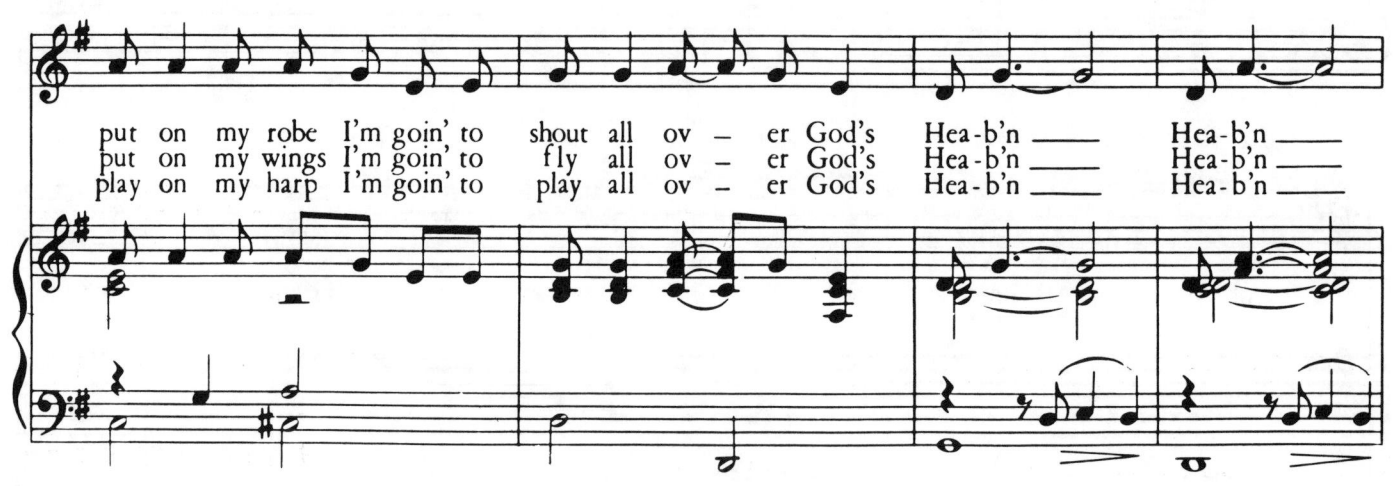

Copyright © 1940 by Edward B. Marks Music Company   Copyright Renewed
International Copyright Secured   Made in U.S.A.   All Rights Reserved
Used by Permission